Table of Contents

Piecing the Blocks

This book contains 24 blocks to make the Star Block Sampler Quilt. Trace the patterns to make the templates, which can be used in either hand or machine piecing. The more accurate you are when tracing your templates, the easier your blocks will fit together.

Pieced Block Templates

Freezer paper is preferred because you can easily see through it to trace the templates, and because the templates can be used several times.

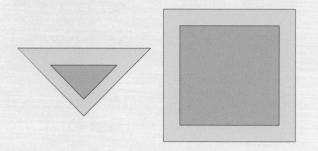

1. Place freezer paper over the drawing of the block. Trace all of the shapes onto the freezer paper; add a ¼" (6mm) seam allowance on all sides. To create exact, clear lines, use a pencil with a thin lead. Number the pieces to keep them in order.

2. Iron the freezer paper onto the right side of your fabric. Remember to set your iron to a no-steam setting.

3. Cut out all shapes and assemble them as shown on the pattern.

Foundation piecing

Foundation piecing is an easy technique to piece your blocks together. In this method, fabric is sewn to the paper foundation following a numerical sequence.

1. Decide how many units the pattern will be divided into.

2. Trace the pattern onto the foundation paper; use a ruler and thin-lead pencil. Copy all of the lines of each unit and add a ¼" (6mm) seam allowance around each unit.

3. Number the foundation paper in the order that the pieces should be sewn together. The more blocks you finish, the easier this will become.

4. Position the fabrics right sides together on the unmarked side of the foundation.

5. Stitch on the sewing line between the numbers using a very small stitch; 1.5 will work on most machines.

6. Continue stitching all of the pieces in numeric order until the block or unit is completed. Trim the fabric so that it is even with the outside line of the foundation. If you have more than one unit for a block, match the units and stitch them together.

7. Keep the foundation paper in place for now; it will help to stabilize the blocks when you sew them together with the sashing.

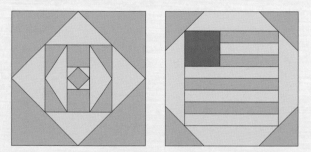

Some blocks can be pieced together as a whole unit.

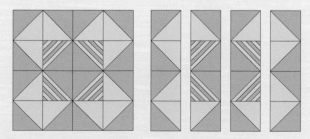

Some blocks need to be pieced together in separate units and then stitched together to make a whole unit.

Materials & Assembly

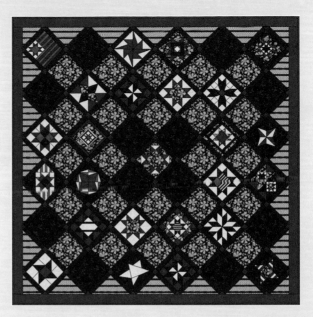

Quilt size: 64"× 64" (163cm × 163cm)
Finished Block Size: 6" × 6" (15cm × 15cm)

FABRIC

TINY PRINTS, TONE-ON-TONES, OR SOLIDS:

1 yd. (91cm) White solid for pieced blocks.

⅓ yd. (30cm) Green Tone-on-Tone for pieced blocks.

1½ yds. (137cm) Large Ivory with Black Floral for pieced and alternate blocks.

1½ yds. (137cm) Small Black with Ivory Print for pieced and alternate blocks.

2 yds. (183cm) Red Tone-on-Tone for pieced blocks, sashing corners, border and binding.

1¼ yds. (114cm) Black Tone-on-Tone for sashing.

¾ yd. (69cm) Stripe for setting and corner triangles.

BACKING:

42" (106.5cm) wide: 4 yds. (365.8cm)
90" (228.6cm) or 108" (274.3cm) wide: 2 yds. (183cm)
Batting: Twin Size.

CUTTING INSTRUCTIONS

Set aside the following cut pieces for your quilt setting and use the rest of the fabrics to piece the star blocks:

Large Ivory with Black Floral: Cut twenty-four 6½" (16.5cm) squares for alternate blocks.

Small Black with Ivory Print: Cut twelve 6½" (16.5cm) squares for alternate blocks.

Red Tone-on-Tone: Cut eighty-four 1½" (3.8cm) sashing corner squares; seven 2½" (6.5cm) strips for border.

Black Tone-on-Tone: Cut one hundred forty-four 1½" × 6½" (3.8cm × 16.5cm) strips for sashing.

Cut five 10" (25.5cm) squares, cut diagonally twice to make twenty side-setting triangles; two 5½" (14cm) squares, one square cut diagonally once and the second square cut diagonally once in mirror image to ensure that the striped print will be horizontal when the four corner setting triangles are stitched into the quilt.

ASSEMBLING THE QUILT TOP

1. Make twenty-five blocks using the instructions on page 4 or follow your favorite piecing method (for this quilt, Peaches & Cream on page 18 was used twice). Arrange the pieced and alternate blocks as they will appear in the quilt.

2. Sew a 6½" (16.5cm) sashing strip to the left edge of each block and to the right edge of the last block in each row.

3. Sew the blocks with sashing strips into rows.

4. Sew sashing strips to 1½" (3.8cm) squares for each sash between the rows of blocks.

5. Sew a side setting triangle to each end of each block row, choosing the correct triangles for each side to ensure the printed stripe lays horizontally in the quilt.

6. Sew the rows together.

7. Sew a corner setting triangle to each of the four corners to complete the inner quilt top.

8. Square up the quilt top, trimming off the extra corners of the sashing squares, and trim any parts of the setting and corner triangles that stick out. Be sure to leave a ¼" (6mm) seam allowance.

9. Sew the border strips together into one strip and then cut: two strips 2½" × 60" (6.5cm × 152.5cm) and two strips 2½" × 64" (6.5cm × 162.5cm).

10. Sew the shorter border strips to the sides of the quilt.

11. Sew the longer border strips to the top and bottom of the quilt.

12. Quilt, bind, and enjoy!

The Blocks

Cartwheels

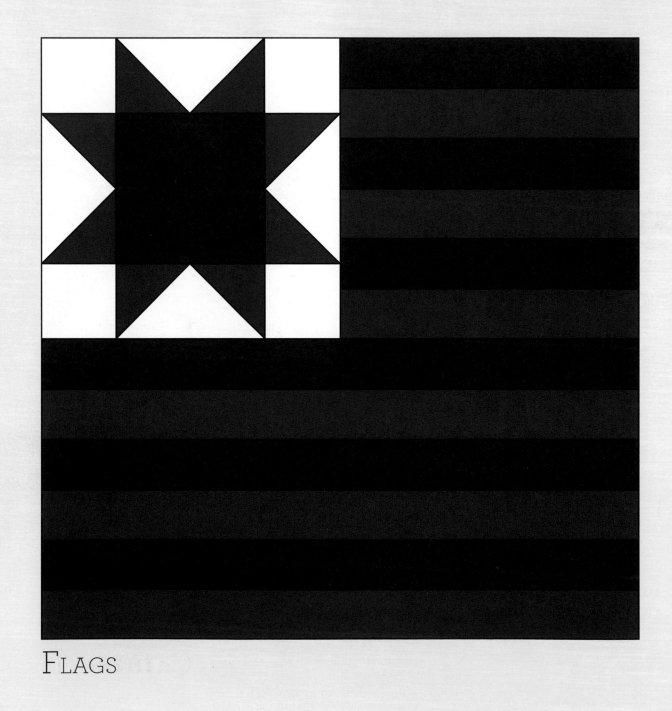

FLAGS

PAPER BLOSSOM

TWISTER

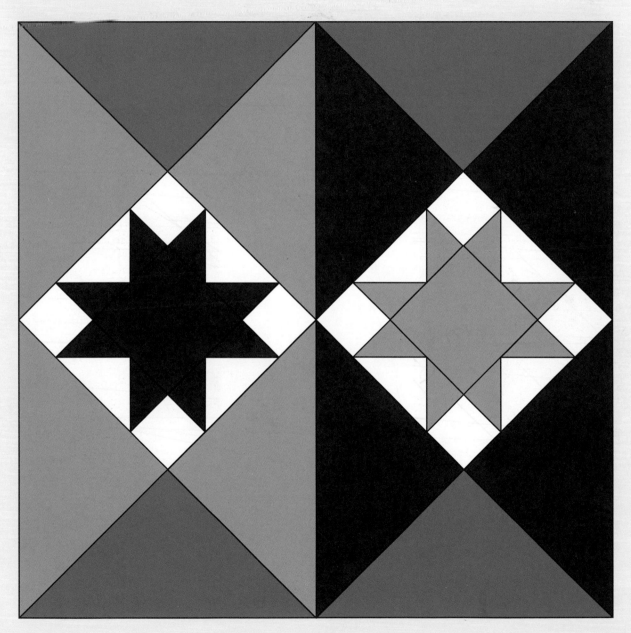

HARLEQUIN

STARBURST

SUGAR & SPICE

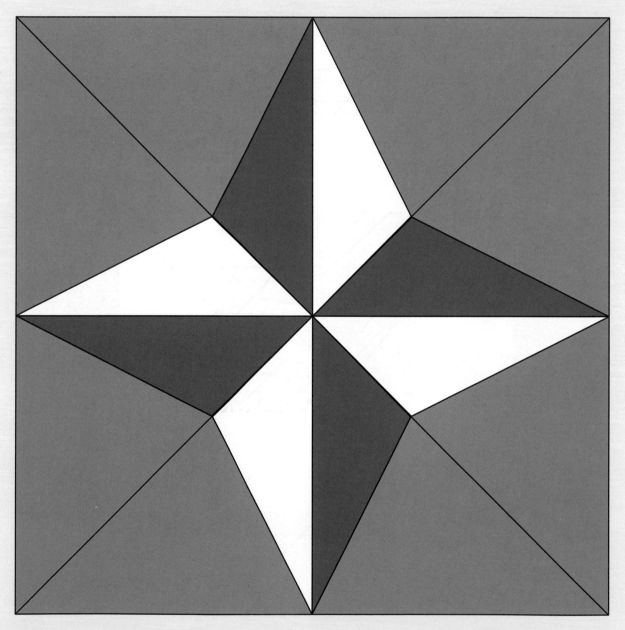

DIAMOND STAR

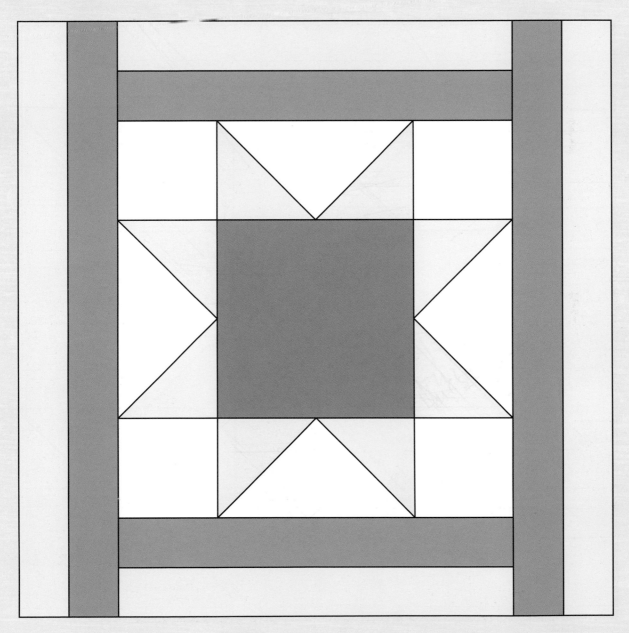

WINDOW BOX

Barbershop

LION'S MANE

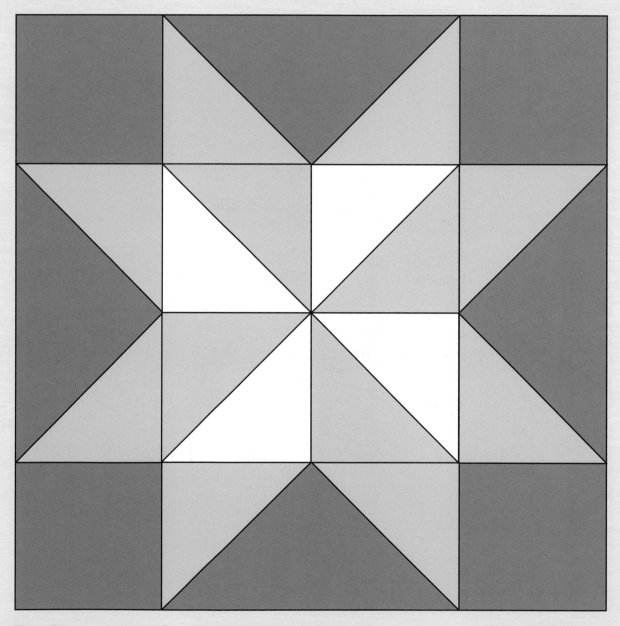

PEACHES & CREAM

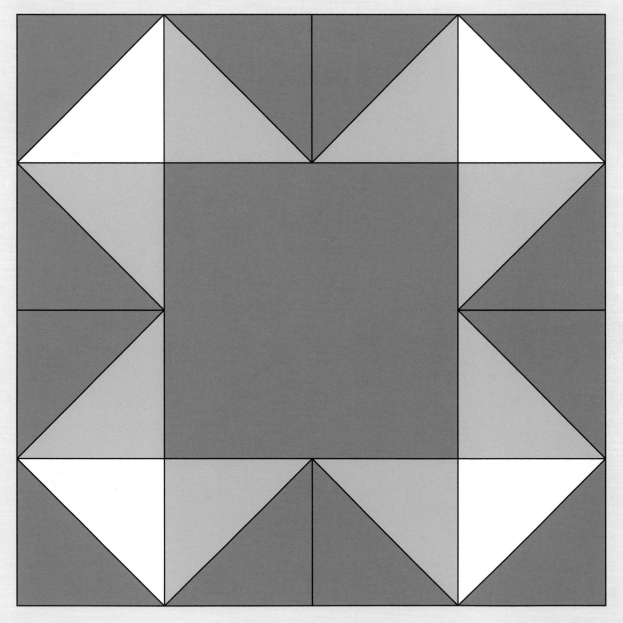

ORIGAMI

EMBRACE

DINNERTIME

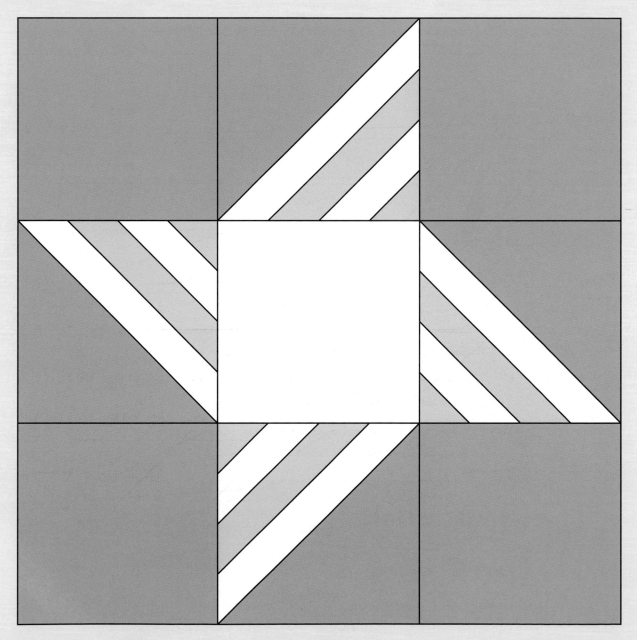

SQUARE DANCE

PATRIOTISM

PERSPECTIVE

PAPER FOLDING

WHIRLPOOL

RIBBON TIED

BEST FRIENDS

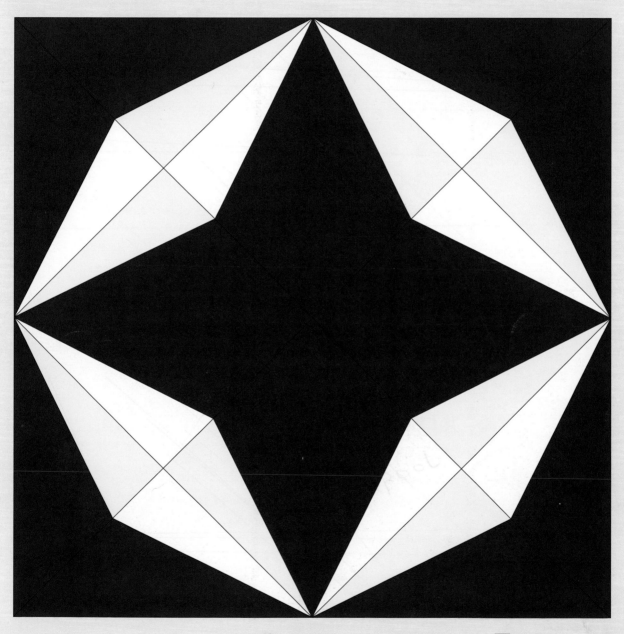

EVOLVING

POINSETTIA